GIANTS

JEREMY BRADSHAW

Introduction by

KEITH SHACKLETON

Contents

ITV BOOKS
in association with
ANGLIA TELEVISION

Introduction

Animals come in many shapes and sizes. This book deals with the giants, the largest animals of their kind. Some are familiar friends like the African Elephant, which is the world's largest land mammal. Elephants can weigh over six tonnes in some cases, which is the weight of eighty people; they tower over us. But there are far smaller giants.

An elephant wouldn't even notice if it trod on the world's largest insect, which is the giant Goliath Beetle. The Goliath Beetle is less than 100 grams in weight, but in relation to other beetles it is huge. It is eight million times the size of the smallest beetle. The world's largest spider would suffer much the same fate under an elephant's foot. It's the Bird-eating Spider of South America, and is about the size of a man's hand. For most people this is quite large enough for a spider, though a closer look at it later on will reveal that this giant is not as terrifying as it first appears.

Why are some animals so large? In the case of a Giraffe, for example, that's quite an easy question to answer. Being the world's tallest land mammal allows it to feed on treetop food that other animals can't reach. But in the case of a whale, the advantages of being 30 metres long and 100 tonnes in weight aren't quite so obvious.

Warm-blooded animals have to maintain their body temperature, even if it's cold outside. Whales, like all mammals, are warm-blooded. The largest of them feed in the freezing water of the Antarctic. They are able to exist in these cold conditions when others couldn't, because a large mammal can keep warmer in this cold environment than a small one. The reason for this is that large animals have less skin, or surface area, in proportion to their size than small ones. If you find this difficult to understand, take a look at an orange. A whole orange has a skin, or peel, all round it. But if you cut it into two halves, then each half would need more skin, or peel, to cover the cut surface. In the same way, two small mammals need more skin to cover them than one large mammal of the same size and weight. By being giant-sized, a whale has proportionately less surface area, and so loses less heat through its skin than a small animal. This is more efficient.

Keith Shackleton with a Blue Whale in the Whale Hall of the British Museum of Natural History. The Blue Whale is the largest animal that has ever lived on Earth. It can weigh up to 150 tonnes, which is the weight of two thousand men. Only creatures that live in water can reach such massive sizes because the water supports their weight. The bodies of land creatures would collapse under the strain of such weight. The massive dinosaurs of prehistory only grew as large as they did because they lived in shallow lakes for much of the time.

There are many other advantages in being a giant. One of the most important is that you are less likely to get attacked by predators. Another is that many giant animals have large brains, and are more intelligent than smaller species.

There are disadvantages in being a giant, too. One problem is how to find and digest the enormous quantities of food needed to keep alive. We'll be looking at the massive whalebone sieves in the mouths of the baleen whales, and the other extraordinary methods of gathering food that have evolved in giants.

One of the most fascinating things about giants is the structure of their bodies. The problem facing them is how to be mobile despite their huge size. Giants that live in the sea have their bulk supported by the water, which buoys them up. But on land it's a different story. Compare an elephant's leg with a horse's, for example, and you will see that the massive bulk of the elephant is supported by heavy, thick legs, each one like a tree-trunk. Next to its bulk, the most extraordinary feature of an elephant is its trunk. To support its huge head, the animal has a very muscular neck, which is too short to allow its mouth to reach the ground. The elephant's nose and upper lips have

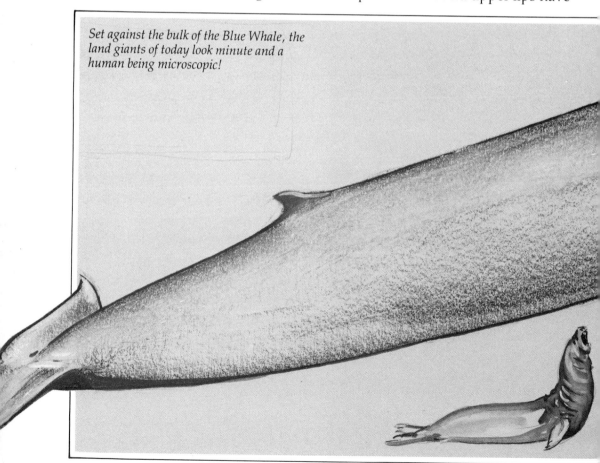

Set against the bulk of the Blue Whale, the land giants of today look minute and a human being microscopic!

Diplodocus *is the longest dinosaur on record. From its skeleton scientists have put together a picture of how it must have looked.* Diplodocus *lived in North America about 140 million years ago.*

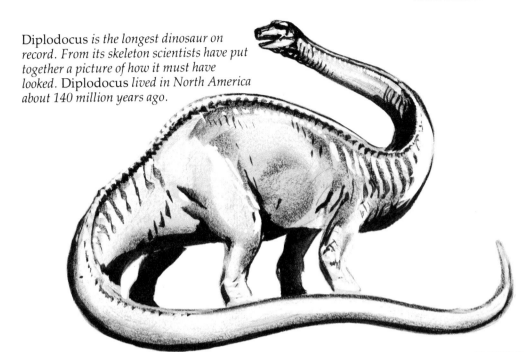

evolved into the trunk as a result. An elephant's trunk is the most amazing device. Equipped with around 30,000 muscles, it can perform at least twenty different types of task.

Man has never treated giant animals well, probably because he feels threatened by their size and sees them as challenging his own supremacy. Many giants are gentle by nature. Some are more aggressive, like the Estuarine Crocodile and the Great White Shark. But to man it doesn't seem to make much difference whether they are dangerous or not. Almost all of them have been ruthlessly killed or hunted at one time or another. Giants suffer very badly if their numbers are reduced by man – more so than many other types of animal. The reason for this is that giants take a long time to replace themselves. A young whale may take at least ten years to reach maturity and thirty years to reach full size. If the adults are all killed, it takes the population a long time to build up again. This has happened with many of the whales, which are now facing extinction.

People often talk about the 'balance' of nature. This 'balance' is not a static thing. Over the years many new creatures have evolved, and many others disappeared, including some colossal giants. In fact, giants are sometimes more vulnerable to the whims of nature than other animals, because they tend to be set in their ways. The dinosaurs are a good example. The largest reptiles the world has ever known, they first appeared during the Triassic period, over 200 million years ago, and ruled the world for millions of years.

The fossil bones of *Diplodocus* were found in rocks near Split Mountain, Utah, USA. This monster measured over twenty-six metres from nose to tail. For a long time scientists couldn't work out how on earth it managed to move about at all. The muscles needed by such a large animal to support its body would have to have been so massive that *Diplodocus* would have collapsed under the weight of them. The answer, it seems, is that *Diplodocus* lived most of its life in shallow water. The water buoyed it up sufficiently for it to stand up and move about.

The age of the giant dinosaurs came to a catastrophic end. We don't quite know why, but there's no doubt that their giant size did not help. One theory is that a giant meteorite hit the Earth and as a result a thick layer of dust hung over the whole world, blocking out the sun's rays. In the resulting darkness, very little vegetation could grow, and so the giants with their enormous appetites starved to death.

Many people do not believe that this is why the dinosaurs died out. They think that it was a change in climate that caused their downfall. Sixty-five million years ago it got colder and the climate more extreme with freezing nights and bitter winters. The dinosaurs were often too cold to search for food and gradually chilled to death.

Fortunately the largest animal the world has ever known is still with us: the Blue Whale, which weighs on average 85 tonnes. In this book you will meet many other giant creatures. Get to know them: if they are not to go the way of the dinosaurs, they will need all our help.

The biggest of them all

The all-time world heavyweights appeared not long after the dinosaurs died out. They're the whales, and many of them are still with us today, though some are in danger of suffering extinction like the dinosaurs. The largest whale of all is the Southern Blue Whale of the southern oceans. It's immense. To give an idea of just how huge this whale is, consider these two facts: a Blue Whale's mouth would quite comfortably house several double-decker buses. Its tongue is the size of an elephant.

The record specimen of a Southern Blue Whale was taken by whalers in South Georgia in the South Atlantic. It was over 33 metres long from its nose to its tail flukes. It wasn't weighed – it's difficult to find a pair of scales big enough for whales – but we can calculate that it was around 150 tonnes. That's an immense weight and it's all the more remarkable when you think that whales and man have the same basic mammalian design. Whales have adapted to the environment unlike any other kind of mammal. Take a look at your own arm and hand. If you were a whale your hand and forearm would be a flipper about three metres long and your upper arm would be short and stubby and inside your body! When it comes to legs, it's a different story. A whale has done away with them almost altogether, to become streamlined like a fish.

As with a fish, the whale's tail provides most of the forward thrust. The bony skeleton of the tail is long and thin like that of other mammals – dogs or cats, for example. But it has two enormous horizontal tail flukes built on to it. They provide all the power, while the front flippers provide control. Mind you, Blue Whales still can't move very fast – their top speed is about 16

kilometres per hour. They don't need to swim very fast. They are so big that they have few natural predators.

Like all mammals, the whale has to breathe air. As a giant, it has to breathe a lot – something like two thousand litres of air at a time. It surfaces to take this in a great gulp through its blow hole – the equivalent of our nostrils, but on the whale's back.

The Blue Whale needs a tonne of food a day on average just to keep alive. The extraordinary thing is that it feeds on very minute forms of life, and in particular on krill. Krill are shrimps which grow up to six centimetres long, and they live in unimaginable quantities in the Antarctic and other cold seas. The surface of the water is sometimes so rich in krill that it becomes like thick, red soup. The Blue Whale sieves this through an extraordinary filter system: its vast mouth is lined with several hundred wing-like plates hanging from the roof of the mouth, one behind the other. The plates are made of *baleen*, or whalebone, which is flexible like plastic. Each of these plates has many thousands of fine hairs or bristles round its edge called *fimbriae*. The whale swims up to the surface and takes a great mouthful of krill 'soup'. It closes its mouth and then pushes the water out with its huge tongue. The water squirts out through the baleen plates, and the krill is caught on the bristly fimbriae.

Krill live only in the colder oceans. As we have seen, a whale's giant size helps it to keep warm. It also has a special 50 centimetre-thick layer of insulation just under the skin, called blubber.

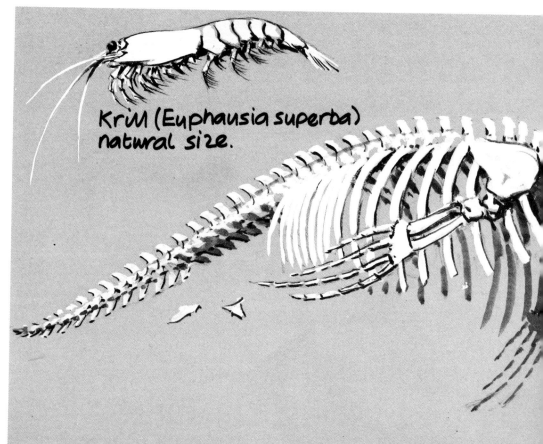

Krill (Euphausia superba) natural size.

Humpback Whales also feed on krill, 'netting' it in a spiral of bubbles.

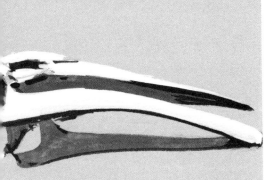

The skeleton of a Blue Whale reveals that its jaws are more than one-third the body length. This enables it to filter the vast quantities of sea water from which it extracts its food. The flipper bones are like the bones of our own hands, but 3 metres long. Note the tiny remnants of the leg bones. The whale is drawn here at 120th of its natural size.

A ten-metre Humpback Whale surfaces in Glacier Bay, Alaska, to take a great mouthful of seawater containing minute krill shrimps.

Whales in danger

Man has always been a hunter, killing animals to satisfy his needs. Giant animals offer large amounts of meat and animal products in one killing, and so man has taken advantage of these harmless creatures. The great whales have suffered terribly as a result. Man has killed whales for over a thousand years. In the old days, it was a very risky business. Anyone who has read *Moby Dick* will know that whales, enraged by harpoons, would sometimes overturn the small rowing boats and kill many whalers. But for the captains it was worth it. The whale oil, boiled down from the blubber, was very valuable: it was used to light lamps before paraffin, gas or electricity were available. Whalebone was used to make items like combs and spoons – there was no plastic then. Finally, there were vast quantities of whalemeat: quantities that could last a community through a whole winter.

For centuries, hunting made little impression on whale stocks. But as man developed advanced technology, he began to slaughter whales mercilessly in every ocean in the world. Today one whale is slaughtered every twenty-five minutes. Advanced sonar and radar location methods, explosive harpoons, and ships that can travel faster than any whale, give these giants of giants little or no chance of getting away.

The motive for this killing is profit. One Blue Whale is worth about £100,000 in oil, meat and whale products. Anyone can kill a whale: it isn't illegal, because they don't belong to anyone. The result is that many species of whale are on the point of extinction. There were once 195,000 Blue Whales swimming the oceans of the world. Now there are just 6,000 left.

The way in which whales are killed is one of the more ghastly aspects of whaling. A grenade-tipped harpoon weighing eighty kilograms is fired into the whale at 90 kph. It explodes inside its body. The whale then takes up to an hour to die from internal bleeding.

Many countries still use whale products extensively. Whale blubber is used to make soap, margarine and cooking fat. The meat is often eaten, or else made into fertiliser. Ambergris from the stomach lining is used in perfumes and face creams. But we now have substitutes, often cheaper ones, for all of these products. There is no longer any excuse for whaling.

The only way to stop the disappearance of so many fine animals is to put a total ban on the killing of whales. Conservationists have now won a sanctuary for whales in the Indian Ocean, and the International Whaling Commission sets limits to the number of each species of whale that may be killed every year. But there are always pirate whalers, who will kill whales illegally for the huge profits, regardless of the effect on the world population of whales.

With the exception of the Killer Whale, these are all endangered species. The slaughter of whales is senseless: the oil and chemical industries today provide cheap substitutes for whale products. There are several organisations working to help the conservation of the whale. They are listed at the end of this book.

Sperm Whale

Right Whale

Bottle-nosed Whale

Killer Whale

Narwhal

Elephant Seals

The seals, the sea lions and walruses are a group of mammals known as Pinnipeds, which means 'fin-footed'. The bodies of Pinnipeds, like those of the whales, have evolved over the ages for a life at sea. But, unlike whales, Pinnipeds leave the sea to breed, because their pups would drown otherwise. The largest of them all is the Elephant Seal and if that were any larger, it probably wouldn't be able to get ashore.

There are two species of Elephant Seal, and they're quite similar. The Northern variety lives around the Pacific islands off the coast of Mexico and Southern California. The Southern form lives in the chilly, sub-Antarctic waters. As we've seen with the whales, the colder the water, the more an animal has to insulate itself; and the larger it is, the better. The Southern Elephant Seal lives in far chillier waters than the Northern, so it has a bigger body, with more insulating blubber.

The largest Elephant Seal on record is a bull seal that measured 6.85 metres in length and weighed 4 tonnes. It was probably 5.5 metres around the waist, though this wasn't actually measured. Bull seals are bigger than cows, which average 1.7 tonnes. Both sexes of this species are way ahead of the next largest Pinniped, the Walrus, which weighs in at 1.3 tonnes.

A 3-tonne bull Elephant Seal rears up and roars aggressively at husband and wife camera team Des and Jen Bartlett, as they make sound recordings.

Elephant Seals are so-called because the bull seal's nose is elongated, forming a trunk-like structure. This inflates when the bull gets aggressive. As the animal grows old, the trunk gets larger, and may be up to 45 centimetres long. When it reaches this size, it actually makes breathing awkward, and has to be held out of the way while the seal is swimming. It seems that the size of this awkward trunk indicates the strength and status of the bearer, rather like the antlers of a stag. A male with a big trunk is usually successful at winning mates, when the seals come ashore for the breeding season.

Seals spend most of their year in and under water. This is their element. They're graceful, highly streamlined swimmers that dive deep in search for their diet of fish and small squid. On land, it's quite a different matter. These heavyweights look like great fat caterpillars, heaving themselves about only with the greatest of effort. They're so very fat because they grow thick layers of blubber before they come ashore to breed.

Breeding is a spectacular event. The bulls roar at each other and engage in murderous-looking fights. The 'beachmasters' – the master bulls – are the biggest, the fattest and the most aggressive of them all. A beachmaster has a harem of up to three hundred females. He has to fight off all other bulls if he's

Walruses live in the coldest of the Arctic seas and haul themselves out frequently to rest in large herds. The second largest Pinniped, the walrus can reach 1.3 tonnes in weight. The tusks, which are long canine teeth, grow up to one metre.

to hold the females. If an invader tries to make off with his females, the beachmaster's first display of aggression is to roar through his trunk, often curling it into the mouth to make it louder. If that doesn't work, the beachmaster rears up so that his body is in an 'L' shape. In this position he stands about two metres tall; he'd look down his trunk at any human. This threatening posture will deter any lesser bull. A bull of equal status requires stronger treatment. One sure way for the defender to topple him is to seize his trunk, which is very painful. The bulls often bite each other on the body, too. But the damage isn't as bad as it might be. Being a giant has its useful side. The extremely thick layer of blubber gives bulls protection against each other's attacks.

Elephant Seal cows give birth ashore. Giants usually have big babies, and the baby Elephant Seal is no exception. The pup is 1.3 metres in length and 35 kilograms in weight. On a diet of fat-rich milk, it grows 30 kilograms a week for the first three weeks. One in five pups never make it to this age; they are victims of the giant beachmasters. As the three-tonne Elephant Seal bulls charge through the colony to drive off intruders, pups get crushed in the hurly burly. It's one of the problems of having such big parents.

Elephant Seals have very few predators. Sperm Whales and Killer Whales may occasionally grab a small one, but by and large Elephant Seals are too much of a mouthful. There is one exception, however. You can probably guess which animal that is. It's *Homo sapiens* – man. Man has slaughtered Elephant Seals mercilessly for their blubber, their meat and for the furs of the newborn pups.

The biggest fish

Say the word 'shark' and most people picture murderous fish patrolling the sun-soaked beaches of the tropics, scything their way amongst bathers with snapping jaws. Though some sharks are dangerous, nothing could be further from the truth for the Whale Shark, which is the largest fish in the world.

Whale Sharks are not as large as whales. They keep themselves to themselves, are rare and seldom hunted, so records of their dimensions are few and far between. The biggest Whale Shark about which we have reliable information was stranded in a fish trap across an estuary in the Gulf of Siam. The local people had never seen anything so big. It completely blocked the channel. It was about 18.5 metres in length and weighed around 40 tonnes. That's a good deal longer than a bus.

There's no mistaking a Whale Shark. Its head isn't pointed like most sharks'. It's flat, and spade-shaped if viewed from the top. The cavernous mouth is right at the front. All other sharks have their mouths tucked underneath their snout.

When humans enter the sea, the home of the great sharks, they must do so on the same terms as other middle-sized marine mammals, and watch out for possible attack.

The Whale Shark is the Earth's largest fish.
It is longer than a bus, and filters 2,000
tonnes of water every hour.

The Whale Shark likes warm, tropical waters, particularly those of the Indian Ocean. It feeds as it swims along, behaving rather like a robot. It travels at about 5 kilometres per hour, opening and shutting its mouth with a monotonous, mechanical regularity, as it takes in the massive gulps of sea water which contain its food.

Like the Blue Whale, the Whale Shark feeds on plankton and also on small fish. Both sieve their meals from the water, but in a different way. The whale has its baleen sieve in its mouth, whereas the Whale Shark has a fine mesh net much further back near its gills. A staggering 2,000 tonnes of water are filtered every hour.

Whale Sharks have almost three thousand teeth, but no one knows what they're for. They certainly aren't used to catch the minute plankton; it would be a bit like trying to use forks to eat soup. They couldn't be used to take large prey animals either, because Whale Sharks can't swallow anything big.

Whale Sharks seem to take little notice of humans. Divers have frequently hitched a ride by holding on to the dorsal fin without the shark appearing to notice. Maybe this isn't surprising. Would an elephant notice a flea on its back? But it is surprising that divers off California have actually held on to the shark's lips and peered into the cavern of its mouth without provoking any reaction. Sadly, the Whale Sharks' lack of sensitivity can be fatal; they regularly collide with ships at sea. Rudyard Kipling, who wrote the *Jungle Book*, was on board a ship in 1905 that accidentally rammed a Whale Shark amidships. He estimated the shark to be 17 metres in length.

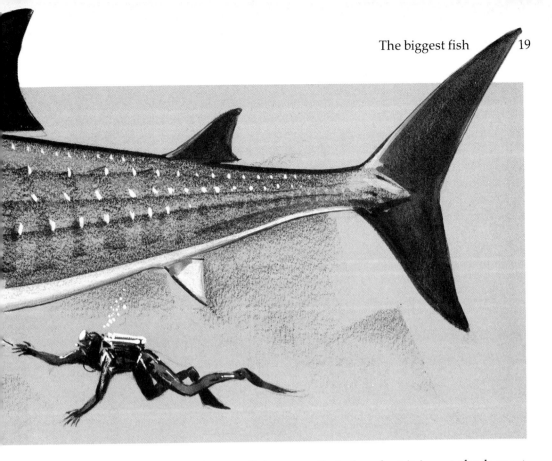

The Whale Shark is the largest fish on earth today, but it is not the largest the world has ever seen. Some thirty million years ago, a giant shark called *Carcharodon megalodon*, or Great Shark, ranged the oceans. It has since become extinct, which is probably rather fortunate for other marine animals. Fossil remains of the Great Shark's teeth were found in an area of California which was once part of the sea bed. They were 15 centimetres long. This is far bigger than the teeth of any shark alive today. A rough estimate suggests that their owner was 22 metres long and weighed up to 45 tonnes. The design of the teeth left no doubts as to what they were used for. The Great Shark was a ferocious killer of giant proportions, which probably attacked and butchered whales and other sharks. One of its descendants is still alive today. It is *Carcharodon carcharias* – the Great White Shark.

The Great White is another record holder. It's the world's largest flesh-eating fish. It also has the distinction of inspiring more terror than any other creature alive today, because of its reputation as a man-eater.

The Great White is unpredictable and its fury is easily aroused. It gets very aggressive, particularly if there's blood in the water, and there's no doubt that it does attack and eat humans; particularly divers and fishermen. On average perhaps fifty people die a year from shark attacks. But one must remember that Great White Sharks have a huge range of prey. Anything up to 3 metres long in the way of fish, porpoises, squids or seals is acceptable. People are quite difficult to catch, particularly in shallow water, and are barely worth the effort. So the Great White is never likely to make us a regular part of its diet.

The giant egg mystery

The Whale Shark and the Great White Shark grow to a very large size. But how do they start out in life? Let's go right back to the beginning of their lives and look at their journey to becoming giants. Some sharks lay eggs. Many more give birth to live young. People always wondered which system the Whale Shark used, but it was only discovered in 1953.

On July 3rd of that year, Captain Odell Freeze of Port Isabel, Texas, was trawling for shrimps out in the Gulf of Mexico when he saw a strange object coming up in the net. It was dark, 36 centimetres long, and purse-shaped. When he cut it

open with his knife, out popped the spade-shaped head of a miniature Whale Shark. Its head shape and spotted back confirmed the identification. This was the first evidence that the Whale Shark laid eggs. It also established another world record for the Whale Shark. The egg is the largest of any living creature on earth.

Where the Whale Shark lays her eggs is still a mystery, but other egg-laying sharks give us a clue as to where we should look. If you've spent any time beachcombing along the seashore then you may well have come across a purse-shaped object about the size of a teabag. They're called mermaid's purses – but it's not money that has fallen out, it's baby sharks that have escaped from them. The occupant was a dogfish.

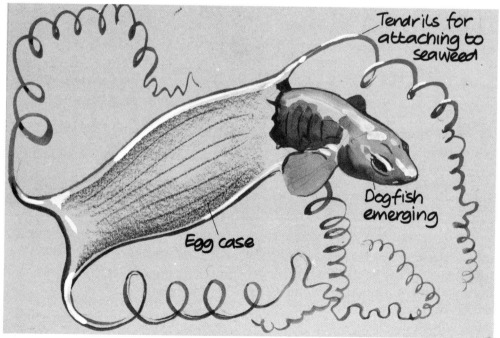

The shark embryo develops in the protection of its egg case, which is attached to fronds of seaweed. The embryo is nurtured by its round yolk sac.

Tendrils for attaching to seaweed

Dogfish emerging

Egg case

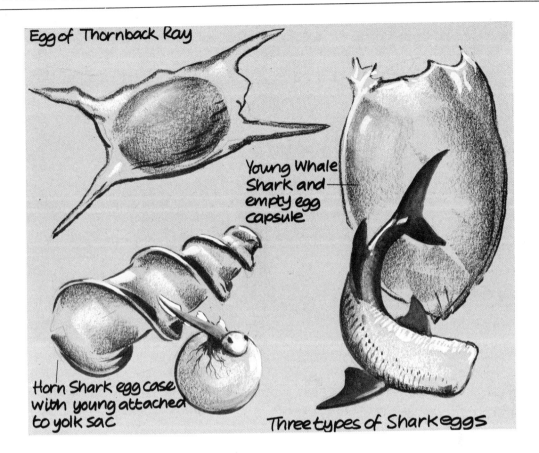

Egg of Thornback Ray

Young Whale Shark and empty egg capsule

Horn Shark egg case with young attached to yolk sac

Three types of Shark eggs

The dogfish that we eat as 'rock salmon' are small sharks which live at the bottom of the sea, feeding on molluscs and crabs. The female lays her eggs in shallow waters close to the shore, in areas with plenty of seaweed. As she lays her eggs, she attaches each one to a frond of seaweed, tying it on by the curly strings, or tendrils, that are attached to all four corners of the mermaid's purse. In the cover of this seaweed jungle, the eggs are safe from predators. For the next eight months, the young shark develops inside. When it has exhausted its supply of yolk, it hatches.

The most extraordinary egg case in the shark world is made by the Horn or Pig Shark, so called after the horn-shaped spines on its back, and its pig-like face. Unlike all other sharks, it lays an egg which is screw-shaped.

Horn Sharks deposit their eggs in rocky crevices. Inside the egg, the embryo feeds on its egg sac for about eleven months. No-one yet knows whether the female screws the egg case into the rock, or just jams it in. But certainly marine biologists have to unscrew them to get them out of their rock crevices. This suggests that the young sharklets developing inside are absolutely safe. There aren't many animals in the sea that have learnt to undo screws!

Insects and spiders

The giants we've been dealing with so far have all had *internal skeletons*. That is to say they have rigid skeletons inside the body to support their weight. The Arthropods – the group of animals which includes the crabs and lobsters, the insects, the spiders and the scorpions – all have outside skeletons, which are called *exoskeletons*. An exoskeleton severely limits the size to which an animal can grow.

The shell of a lobster, or the black-and-yellow body casing of a wasp, is its exoskeleton. A lobster's or a wasp's legs are also encased in a hard outside skeleton. These exoskeletons are essentially tubes of hard material. Small tubes are light and extremely strong for their weight. A cardboard tube, for example, can take quite a strain before it bends and snaps. But large tubes have to be very thick if they are to be strong. As a result they are extremely heavy, and this is one of the main reasons why insects, in particular, do not grow to a large size; their exoskeletons would be so heavy that the insects could hardly move, let alone fly.

The heaviest insect in the world is only 100 grams in weight. It's the Goliath Beetle of Equatorial Africa. At only 120 millimetres from the tip of its horns to the back of its abdomen, it may not seem a giant. But it is when you compare it with the smallest beetle. The Goliath Beetle is eight million times larger! It is not the world's fastest mover – far from it, in fact. These beetles are sluggish in their movements, and there's a very good reason for this.

The Bird-eating Spider. This hairy Trinidadian species preys on small lizards and grasshoppers. The long hairs act as a parachute if the spider falls out of a tree.

The Goliath Beetle is the world's largest insect. It weighs only 100 grams but it is eight million times larger than the world's smallest beetle.

Unlike all the giants we've looked at so far, insects do not have lungs or gills, and cannot breathe very efficiently. Insects rely on a process called *diffusion* to get oxygen to their muscles. Diffusion is a slow process. You can get an idea of diffusion in action if you put some sugar into a cup of cold water. If you don't stir the water, it takes a long time for the sugar to dissolve and for you to be able to taste it. Diffusion is the process by which the sugar slowly distributes itself throughout the water.

As far as insects are concerned, it is oxygen that has to diffuse through the air into their bodies. This is a slow process at the best of times, and the larger the insect, the more difficult it is. Goliath Beetles can never get enough oxygen to their large muscles to indulge in strenuous exercise. They bumble about like huge armoured tanks.

When it comes to the spiders, it's a different story altogether. There's something about spiders that humans find repellent. A recent survey revealed that one of people's greatest fears was that a spider would crawl into their bed or down their neck.

The largest spiders in the world live in South America and the Caribbean. These giant spiders belong to a group known as the Bird-Eating Spiders. The largest is larger than a man's hand. The giant member of the family we're going to describe here is the Avicularia Bird-Eating Spider. Like others of its kind, it is a hunter; it does not build webs to catch its prey, but either runs it

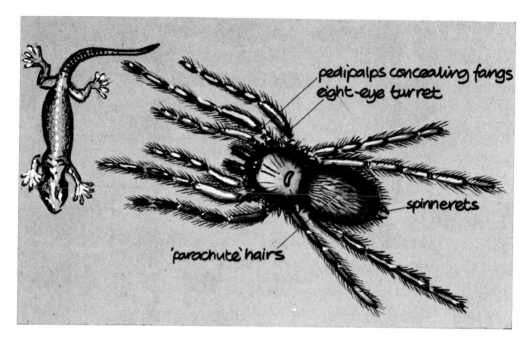

Theraphosa blondi is the largest Bird-eating Spider in the world.

down or ambushes it. It usually attacks small lizards and grasshoppers. Naturalists once thought it attacked and killed humming birds as they hovered in front of flowers, but this is not the case. Bird-Eating Spiders restrict their bird eating to the occasional nestling. Death is brought about by stabbing with sharply pointed fangs, followed by the injection of a mild poison.

Large spiders such as the Bird-Eaters are not sluggish like the giant beetles. The reason for this is that spiders have organs under their abdomens which work like lungs: the spider can breathe in and out through them. As a result, Bird-Eating spiders can move very swiftly if necessary.

Very few animals prey on the Bird-Eating Spider. This is not because of its size, but because the spider has a very effective protection, which predators soon learn to avoid. It's the spider's spines which defend it so well. If they touch the human skin, they cause intense irritation and even partial paralysis. One zoo keeper who touched a Bird-Eating Spider by mistake was temporarily paralysed. Fortunately he managed to shake the spider off. Incidentally, the spider's venom is said to be no more poisonous than that of a wasp sting.

Bird-Eating Spiders occasionally fall out of trees while climbing about in search of prey. Being such large spiders, the chances are that they would burst if they hit the ground at speed. Evolution has prepared the spider for accidents like this, by giving it long body hairs. These stream outwards, acting as a parachute to slow the giant spider's fall.

Crocodiles, dragons and tortoises

With the passing of the dinosaurs, the reptiles' domination of the earth was over, but they didn't all die out. Several types of reptile which were alive in the age of the dinosaurs survived, and one group of them evolved into the largest living reptiles. They're the crocodiles, which still somehow look prehistoric.

The largest of all the crocodiles is the Estuarine, or Saltwater, Crocodile. The males weigh around 450 kilograms. Average length is 5 metres, but they can grow up to 9 metres.

First of all, let's find out just what the advantages are for a crocodile in being so large. The answer lies in the crocodile's way of life. It kills its prey by

The Saltwater Crocodile is the most colossal crocodile of all. It lives in mangrove swamps and estuaries throughout Northern *Australia, Malaysia and the Indian sub-continent. It preys on fish and waterbirds, livestock and small mammals.*

stalking it, usually from underwater, but sometimes in the cover of the reeds. The crocodile may seize its prey in its jaws immediately. Or it may swing its body round, so that its enormous tail lashes the victim, knocking the feet from under it and hurling it into the river. A big crocodile is more successful and can take large prey. It therefore has to feed less often.

The second big advantage in being large is in temperature regulation. Crocodiles are not warm-blooded. But they must still keep their body temperature within four degrees of 25° centigrade. A bigger body gains and loses heat less quickly than a smaller one. Its temperature is more stable, and so the crocodile doesn't get cold and sluggish and doesn't overheat so often as smaller reptiles do.

Crocodiles are amphibious animals, but their great bulk coupled with their prehistoric design means that they walk extremely awkwardly on land. They sometimes look as if they can barely support their own weight, as they waddle along on their short, stiff legs. That's not to say that Estuarine Crocodiles can't move in a hurry. They can, but not on their legs. They 'belly run', sliding on their bellies with their legs spread out sideways.

The biggest of all the lizards is better adapted to move on land. It is a monitor lizard called the Komodo Dragon. It doesn't actually breathe fire, but it is still an ancient and dangerous-looking animal which lives only on the remote Sunda Islands of Komodo, Rintja, Padar and Flores in the Pacific Ocean. It's the largest land carnivore on the islands, and in the absence of competition, it has grown to gigantic proportions, exceeding three metres in length.

Gigantic species of animals often develop on islands. On the Galapagos, 6,000 kilometres east of Komodo, there are two types of giant reptiles. There is the Marine Iguana, which is a large lizard with a crest of scales down its back, and the Giant Tortoise. Giant Tortoises are the larger of the two. They're so big that a man can ride them. They're 170 kilograms in weight and over one metre high. The Giant Galapagos Tortoise is a gentle herbivorous giant that lives to the ripe old age of two hundred years.

The Giant Tortoise of the Galapagos is a gentle, slow moving giant until it comes to courtship, when the male stirs into action.

The Komodo Dragon is the world's largest lizard. Lizards have their legs set out to the side; this limits their maximum weight.

The giant reptiles

The reptilian order of Crocodilia consists of the crocodiles, the caimans, the alligators and the gavials. There's a myth that crocodiles live in Africa and alligators live in America, but while this is broadly true, it is not entirely accurate. In addition to their African range, crocodiles occur in south-eastern Asia, Australia and parts of America. Almost all alligators live in the Americas, but for some unknown reason, one species is found in the Yangtze River valley in China. Closely related to alligators are the caimans. Caimans are confined to the northern parts of South America, mainly the Amazon valley. Gavials live in Nepal and India.

The word 'crocodile' had small beginnings. It comes from the Greek *krokodilos*. *Krokodilos* is the word the Greeks use to describe the small wall lizard that scuttles around outside their houses and in their gardens. When they encountered crocodiles for the first time, probably on the Nile, they used the same word for them because of their similar design. Alligator comes from the Spanish *el largato*, which means 'lizard'. Gavial comes from the

(Above) The crocodile: a narrow snout with the teeth of the lower jaw prominent.

(Below) The alligator: a broad snout with the upper jaw teeth lying outside.

Hindustani word *gharial*. In fact, many people use this name rather than gavial.

The best way to tell members of the Crocodilia apart is to have a look at the jaws. With the crocodiles, nearly all the teeth are visible, even when the jaws are closed. The fourth tooth back from the snout in the lower jaw is longer than the others, and sticks up.

The alligators have a broader muzzle, and a bony ridge between the nostrils. Their lower teeth are hidden by those of the upper jaw when the mouth is shut. The long fourth tooth is hidden too, for it fits into a socket in the top jaw. It can sometimes be seen, for if it grows too long it can pierce right through the upper jaw, and stick out.

The caimans look rather like the alligators, except that they have no ridge between the nostrils, and their teeth tend to be longer and more pointed.

The slim muzzle of the gavials has been likened to a saucepan handle. They eat fish, impaling them on their formidable array of teeth – twenty-eight in the upper jaw, twenty-six in the lower.

The expression 'crocodile tears' comes from the belief that crocodiles weep in grief when they are devouring their victims. It's unlikely that the croc can feel any remorse. Do you when you eat your meals?

(Above) The caiman: short, broad jaws with razor-sharp teeth.

(Below) The gavial: a very slender snout, packed with teeth to catch fish.

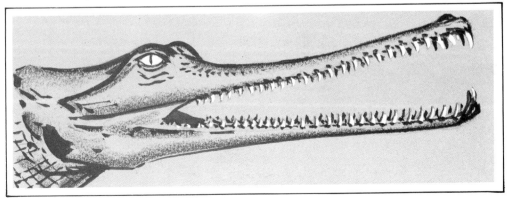

Record-breaking birds

Direct descendants of the dinosaurs are alive and well and living throughout the world. Believe it or not, dinosaurs are thought to be the ancestors of today's birds.

It all started around one hundred and fifty million years ago, when one of the many dinosaurs that roamed the earth began to grow feathers. The feathers were probably for insulation, to enable it to keep warm – a problem which defeated so many of the dinosaurs. As the years went by, the feathers

A pair of Ostriches stand head-and-neck above a Wildebeest on the plains of the Serengeti, Tanzania. The cock is on the right.

on the arms and the tail developed in such a way as to allow this small dinosaur to glide and later to fly. Millions of years later, its descendants have evolved into the great variety of birds we have today. The giants among them aren't so large as the dinosaurs, and there are very good reasons for this. Birds are of two basic types: those that fly and those that don't. Let's look at the flying ones first.

The largest flying birds are rarely more than 14 kilograms in weight. This is just about the upper weight limit for take-off and powered, flapping flight. The bustards, the Mute Swan, the condors and the pelicans approach this maximum flying weight.

To get up into the air, a heavy bird has to flap hard. The power to beat its wings downwards for lift-off comes from the chest, or *pectoral* muscles. The bigger the bird, the larger and stronger muscles it needs to power its take-off. But pectoral muscles are themselves very heavy, and there comes a point when however much the bird increases its pectoral muscles it just won't get off the ground. If the bird weighs more than 14 kilograms, it can only fly with the greatest difficulty.

The heaviest flying birds today are the Kori and Arabian Bustards of Africa. The cock birds are heavier than the females and sometimes even exceed 14 kilograms. These bustards fly only when threatened, because it requires so much energy to take to the wing. To take off they run purposefully along the ground flapping their huge wings, which span 2.6 metres. The beats are powerful, but the birds take their time to get into the air. It's not surprising with all that weight on board!

Bustards fly as little as possible; they much prefer to run away from danger. This strategy for survival has been taken one step, or perhaps one should say stride, further by the Ostrich.

The ancestors of the Ostrich were most certainly flying birds, but for some reason they gave it up, probably because they found they no longer needed to fly to escape predators. Without the weight limit that flight imposes, Ostriches have become the world's largest living birds. A mature cock bird would look down its nose (or beak!) at you. It averages about 2.4 metres in height and 126 kilograms in weight. Heights of 2.7 metres and weights of 157 kilograms have been reported but not confirmed.

If they do spot danger, Ostriches can certainly get a move on. They can run at 50 kilometres per hour for up to half an hour, which is enough to tire most hunters. It's the massive leg muscles which make it all possible. They are almost bare of feathers, to stop them overheating while on the run.

One characteristic that the birds still have in common with the dinosaurs is that they lay eggs, though they are slightly different. It comes as no surprise that Ostrich eggs are the largest of any bird (the Whale Shark's is the largest in the animal kingdom). Ostrich eggs are about 18 centimetres long and around 1.6 kilograms in weight. That's the equivalent of twenty hens' eggs! But the extraordinary thing is that *in proportion,* the eggs are the *smallest* of any bird. For most birds, their egg is between one-tenth and one-fifteenth of their own body weight. In theory, the Ostrich egg should be at least 7 kilograms.

There is a possible explanation of why the Ostrich egg is six times smaller than it should be: the shell of a larger egg would be too thick for the chicks to peck their way out. As it is, they often take several hours to get out of their eggs. When they finally emerge, they're 31 centimetres tall. Within a month they can travel as fast as their gigantic parents.

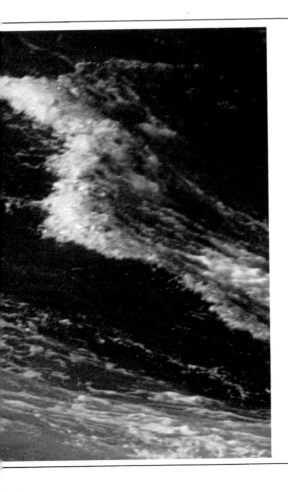

The back of an Arabian Bustard provides a convenient perch for a Carmine Bee-eater in the Danakil Desert of Ethiopia. Bustards are the largest flying birds but only fly when necessary.

The Wandering Albatross soars in the winds of the Roaring Forties and Furious Fifties, above some of the worst seas in the southern hemisphere. Its wingspan may reach 3.6 metres.

The gliders

The Wandering Albatross has the largest wingspan of any bird alive today. The greatest span recorded is around 3.6 metres. This is quite a bit wider than its closest rivals for the title. The Marabou Stork has a span of 2.8 metres. The Trumpeter Swan may reach 3 metres, and the Andean Condor 3.2 metres.

The Wandering Albatross is aptly named, spending much of its time wandering the southern oceans, often in the latitudes of the Roaring Forties and the Furious Fifties –

some of the stormiest regions in the world.

You may have spotted that the albatross's wing is very like a glider's wing. This is no coincidence. A long thin wing is the most efficient one for gliding. The albatross spends most of its time gliding over the ocean, making use of winds rising over the waves to gain height.

The albatross hardly ever flaps its wings unless it has to. It sets its wings and soars upward into the wind to gain height, until the headwinds begin to slow it down. At the top of this climb, it turns and then accelerates downwind, almost touching the ocean before turning to

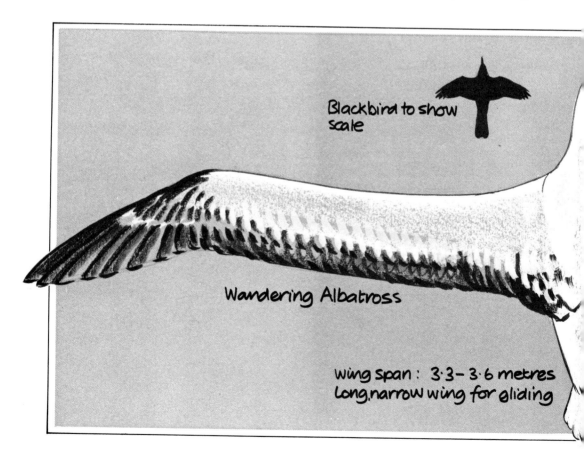

Blackbird to show scale

Wandering Albatross

Wing span : 3·3 – 3·6 metres
Long, narrow wing for gliding

ascend again.

There are, however, vital differences between a glider's wing and an albatross's. A glider's wing is completely rigid. The albatross, and in fact all birds, can vary the shape and span of their wings, and choose just the right shape for the gusting wind conditions.

The Andean Condor closely approaches the Wandering Albatross in wingspan. The record spread for an Andean Condor is 3.2 metres, but its real claim to fame is the great area of the wings and tail. The condor has the greatest 'sail' area of any bird on earth today. This is necessary for its way of life.

Condors are vultures that live in the main in the high Andes Mountains of South America. Like all vultures, the condor feeds on carrion. Carrion is pretty thin on the ground in mountain areas like the Andes, and the condor has to fly big distances to find it. Its great sail area enables it to fly those distances with the minimum of effort.

To travel a long distance, the condor circles in an upcurrent of air, which is often a *thermal*, or rising column of hot air caused by the warmth of the sun. It climbs several thousand metres at a time, and sets its course. It can then glide for 25 or 30 kilometres, losing height all the time but reaching speed of 100 kilometres per hour.

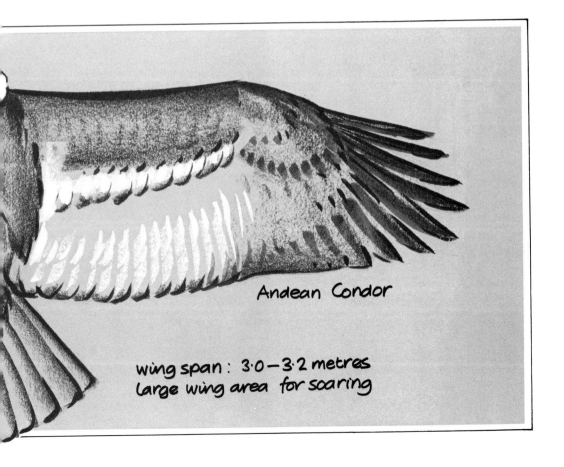

Andean Condor

wing span: 3.0 — 3.2 metres
large wing area for soaring

Land giants

When Europeans first heard about the Giraffe in the Middle Ages, they couldn't believe that it was a real animal. They reckoned that it was too tall to be true, and must be a mythical beast like a unicorn.

Giraffes are the world's tallest living land animals. The bull Giraffes are largest. They average 5 metres in height from their hooves to their horns, which means they can see over a double-decker bus. They weigh in at over a tonne. Cows average 4.4 metres and are just over half a tonne.

The Giraffe has evolved so that it can stretch up to about 6 metres, using its 45 centimetre-long tongue to hook down branches and leaves otherwise out of

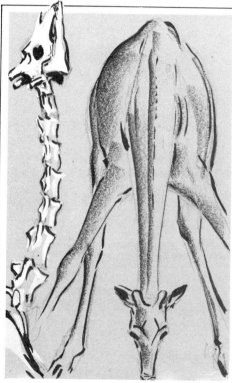

A Giraffe has the same number of neck vertebrae as man – but they're all much larger! When the head is lowered to drink it suddenly changes from being the highest point of the body to the lowest. A network of spongy blood vessels near the brain asborbs the initial surge of blood to the head, and a unique system of valves in its arteries stops the blood pressure building up.

reach. Giraffes specialise in feeding on acacia trees in many parts of Africa. Acacias have 6 centimetre-long thorns along the branches to protect the leaves. But the Giraffes can cope with this, even though it must be a bit like eating spinach and barbed wire. Their lips are prehensile and thorn-proof. The elephant is the only other ground-living animal able to feed at this level.

The cover of this book shows a fully grown female African Elephant charging at the camera. The elephant puts on this terrifying display to frighten away intruders. She makes herself look even more formidable by fanning out her ears and raising up her sharp tusks. Notice the way she holds her sensitive trunk out of the way. In all probability, she will not press home her attack: elephants are gentle and, above all, intelligent giants.

Bull elephants are the larger sex. They measure 3.2 metres at the shoulder on average, and weigh around 5.5 tonnes. Cow elephants average 2.6 metres and 2.5 tonnes. Several tonnes is a huge weight for an elephant's bones to

Reticulated Giraffe tower over the African savannah in northern Kenya.

support. But, over millions of years, the skeleton has evolved to this end. The elephant has legs built like pillars, so that the strain on the joints is at a minimum. The pressure on them must be vast, as it must also be between foot and the ground. A special springy pad cushions the sole of the foot against this pressure.

African Elephants live in the heat of the tropics or near-tropical regions, and overheating can be a problem. It's the opposite of the problem the whale has, which is to keep warm. With their relatively small surface area, elephants have big problems in *losing* enough heat. The elephant solves this problem with its massive ears. These increase the elephant's surface area by about one-third, and are so richly supplied with blood that they cool the elephant down, just as a car radiator cools a car engine. By flapping them, the elephant can bring its temperature down by five degrees. Elephants also wallow and bathe regularly to cool themselves, often after drinking. Elephants have to drink every day. They can't live without drinking regularly because they sweat so much to keep cool. Their daily intake of water is around 100 litres.

An elephant's food intake is about 130 kilograms of food a day. A huge variety of plant material is acceptable because an elephant's teeth are so strong that it can chew branches and even the roots of trees. There are powerful grinding molar teeth on each side of the jaw. The largest of these is 21 centimetres long, with a surface the size of your hand.

Although the elephant chews its food very efficiently, it still has to digest what is often very woody, fibrous food. This is pretty high on roughage, but low on nutrients like protein and carbohydrate. To get these, the elephant has to digest its food for a long time in its stomach, brewing it up with digestive juices for about three days. Three days' worth of digesting food is about 400 kilograms in weight, which the elephant has to cart about inside everywhere it goes. That's another reason why the elephant has to be a giant.

At birth, baby elephants are the same weight as a heavyweight boxer – about 90 kilograms. Their mothers look after them devotedly, within a family herd made up of several grandmothers, mothers, aunts, teenagers and babies. Elephants are sociable animals and the calves are constantly played with and protected. If danger threatens, the females will gather into a defensive circle, with the calves inside. This forms a formidable 'elephant wall' between the calves and the danger. Being the largest of land giants, they have little to fear – except man. Today, man regards tusks as a valuable commodity to be hoarded like gold or diamonds. Elephants are now killed by poachers with automatic weapons throughout their dwindling range in Africa, despite strenuous efforts made by game wardens and rangers. These magnificent creatures are among the many threatened by human greed.

The 4.5 tonne Indian Elephant is the second largest land mammal in the world after the African species. It grows up to 3 metres at the shoulder. It is a highly intelligent animal that is trained to work in parts of India, Sri Lanka, Nepal and Burma. It is particularly useful for logging. Each trained elephant has its personal mahout or driver.

The incredible trunk

The fact is that elephants pack an awful lot into their trunks: around 30,000 muscles control it. Some of them have to be very strong: the trunk weighs 200 kilograms. Other muscles are very small. There are also many millions of nerves. All in all, the elephant's trunk is one of the most sensitive organs in the animal kingdom and can carry out many different functions.

Tall animals have to have some means of reaching the ground. The giraffe's long neck enables it to do this, but you might say that the elephant's trunk is a better solution to the problem. It allows the neck to be short and strong, and so support a massive head, which means a larger brain, larger teeth and more powerful jaws to crush and chew tough food. In short, it helps the elephant to be the intelligent and efficient giant it is.

The best way to describe the elephant's trunk is to compare it with a sensitive, free-moving and highly adaptable limb. It can be a hand, an arm, a hose, a wind vane, a windspeed indicator, a nose, a trumpet, a weapon and a snorkel. It is sensitive to touch and scent, and can be used in courtship and social communication. Without it, an elephant has little chance of survival.

When an elephant is taking one of its regular drinks, the trunk sucks up a bucketful of water at a time and then squirts it into the mouth. The trunk cannot be used like a straw, incidentally: remember that the trunk is the elephant's *nose*. But it can be used to spray water all over the elephant's back to cool it down.

When it comes to feeding, the trunk can reach anything from ground level up to five and a half metres. It can tear down whole branches, uproot trees and strip them of bark. But it can be a very delicate organ, too. The elephant can pick up something the size of a peanut with the finger-like structures at the tip.

An elephant always explores its close surroundings with its trunk, smelling and touching anything unfamiliar. It can find out what's happening at longer distances by putting its trunk upright, in order to get a clearer scent. If it's in the correct position downwind, an elephant can scent other animals three kilometres away.

The elephant makes a wide range of sound through its trunk. It can trumpet, it can scream and it can snort. It also uses it for more direct communication. Elephants touch and feel each other in a surprisingly human way. They use their trunks for reassuring and greeting. A young elephant greets a larger stranger by placing its trunk in the stranger's mouth. Within the family herd, the grandmothers, the mothers and the calves are constantly touching each other with their trunks.

The tip of an African Elephant's trunk has two little 'fingers' which can pick up something as small as a peanut. The Asiatic Elephant has only one finger. Elephants can use their trunks for many different purposes.

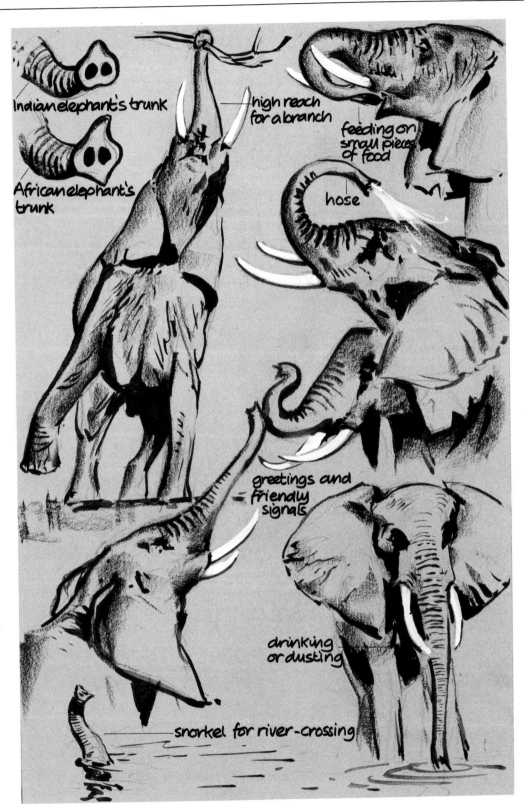

Indian elephant's trunk

African elephant's trunk

high reach for a branch

feeding on small pieces of food

hose

greetings and friendly signals

drinking or dusting

snorkel for river-crossing

Giant ape

The Gorilla is the giant member of the ape family, of which man is a member. Other apes include the Chimpanzee, the Gibbon, the Orang Utan, the Gorilla and ourselves.

Gorillas live in groups of about a dozen or so, headed by a very large 'silverback' male. Silverback males are so-called because their backs turn from black to a silver-grey, as a sign of their maturity and dominance. Silverbacks are immense. They can weigh as much as 275 kilograms and stand 1.8 metres tall. The ridge of cartilage on the tops of their heads adds greatly to their impression of height. A silverback male seldom stands upright, but it is no less awesome for this.

Gorillas are very rare and live in the very thick forests of Central and Western Africa. There are two types. The Lowland Gorilla lives in the forests of the Congo River. The Mountain Gorilla lives in the area of the Virunga Volcanos that straddle the Rwanda-Zaïre border.

Most of a Gorilla's life is spent feeding on the ground: they don't often climb trees because the branches might break under their weight. They're strict vegetarians, including in their diet vines, giant celery, wild thistles, nettles, fruit, ferns and roots. Gorillas have never been seen to drink, which is hardly surprising. Their rainforest home is always dripping with dew, rain and condensation.

Like many vegetarian giants we have looked at, Gorillas spend a lot of time eating during their daily routine. Gorillas make nests of vegetation on the ground which they sleep in. After dawn, they 'lie in' for an hour or two until they get up. The morning is spent ripping up great handfuls of giant celery or vines, to eat. Lunchtime is spent resting. Then the group feeds until nightfall when it goes to sleep.

Like ourselves, Gorillas live in family groups. The silverback male leader is usually at least ten years old. He dominates the other members of the group, which consists of females, juveniles and young. He makes almost all the decisions. He protects the group, too. If an intruding male, or a threatening animal like man appears, he roars or hoots at them. He will then tear up the undergrowth and throw branches into the air. He may even beat his chest with slightly cupped hands. If this display has no impact, the silverback charges, crashing through the undergrowth. Like elephants, Gorillas seldom go through with it; the sight of the giant's charge is enough to send other Gorillas on their way.

A male silverback Gorilla in the Kahuzi-Biega National Park, Zaire. Gorillas are usually peaceful giants that spend their lives in thick forest, eating massive quantities of wild thistles, vines, giant celery, fruit, ferns and roots.

Tail piece

There's one animal that we've been talking about a lot, but that we have not yet classified as a giant. It's ourselves – the human race. We are giants because we have a giant ability to put our large brains into action. Our large brain makes us rather different from many other animals, including the other apes. Its larger size, and special design, have given us a unique intelligence.

That's not to say that we are more intelligent than all other species. Many of the whales, for example, have far larger brains than we have. The Sperm Whale has the largest brain in the animal kingdom, and there's every reason to suppose that the Sperm and other whales are very intelligent. The Humpback Whale, for example, has a very complex 'song' or language with which it communicates.

The difference between ourselves and other intelligent creatures is that they have not been able to use their intelligence to develop technology. It is technology which gives us our giant status. Technology has produced our tools, cars, computers, weapons, washing machines, tractors, and so on. It has enabled us to do many complicated things and to conquer almost every environment on earth, from the top of Everest to the bottom of the sea. It allows us to imitate anything any other animal can do, including the giants.

Take the Blue Whales and the Elephant Seals, for example. Their huge size means that they can operate efficiently and keep warm as they exploit the great quantities of krill, fish, or squid in the Antarctic or sub-Antarctic waters of the Southern Ocean. Man has learned how to do the same. In ships with heating, diesel engines, and kitchens on board, using nets, he can go anywhere whales or seals go to catch krill or fish in greater quantities.

Another advantage of giant size is the safety it offers. Few predators will attack full-grown elephants, Giraffe, or Whale Sharks, for example. Few predators attack us, either. Our weapons, and the poisonous chemicals we can produce make us safe from the attack of most other animals.

Man has done more than just defend himself against wildlife; he has worked actively to dominate it with his technology. There's no doubt that the giants in the animal kingdom have suffered more than most. The great whales have suffered directly, elephants have suffered both directly and indirectly, providing a classic example of Man versus Giant. Elephants used to roam a good proportion of the thick forests of Africa. They fed in an area, bulldozing more trees over as the food supply diminished. When that region of forest was exhausted, the elephants would move on to another area where the forest was not so heavily used. They might not return to the first area until twenty years later, when the trees had had a chance to recover. In this way, although they did considerable damage to an area while they were feeding in it, in the long term they did no lasting damage to the forest at all.

Today, the elephants are very restricted in their movements. Many have nowhere to go, because so much of Africa's ancient forests have been taken over by mankind, cut down to make way for agriculture and cities. We, the giants of technology, have found ways to knock down the trees faster than the elephants ever did, and after we have pulled up the stumps, and ploughed the land and fertilised it to grow our crops, the forest will never return. Meanwhile, the elephants ruin the last remaining areas of forest with their feeding.

Perhaps we can learn something from the elephants. In their natural state, almost destroying an area, then moving on while it recovers, they're all right, just so long as there's enough habitat. Man is a giant who over-exploits not just small areas of land but most of the earth. We ought to leave it to recover, because if we destroy it completely, there will be nowhere for us to go: unless we abandon ship completely, and go to another planet.

If we used our giant brains, we'd realise that we must not take over the whole of the world for human use. We should leave some of it for the other animals. That way all the giants will have a better chance of survival, ourselves included.

If you want to help in the fight to save the world's endangered animal giants and other endangered species, contact one of these organisations:

Friends of the Earth
9, Poland Street,
London W.1.
01-434 1684

Royal Society for the Protection of Birds
The Lodge,
Sandy,
Bedfordshire SG19 2DL
(SAE Please)
Sandy 80551

World Wildlife Fund
11-13, Ockford Road,
Godalming GU7 1QU
Godalming 20551

Greenpeace,
36, Graham Street,
London N.1.
01-251 3020
(Marine Mammals only)

Young People's Trust for Endangered Species
19, Quarry Street,
Guildford,
Surrey GU1 3EH
Guildford 39600